College Uncensored
By: Joshua Hicks

Copyright 2019 by Joshua Hicks

Library of Congress Cataloging-in-Publication Data

ISBN: 978-0-578-49974-1

Athletes Remorse Publishing

This book is dedicated to my mother and father, who have always been there for me. Who taught me to be the man I am today; I will forever be grateful to have you both in my life.

To my family members, thank you for being along for this journey. It really takes a village to raise a child. I love you all.

To my squad, you all know who you are. We've been through a lot through the years and you guys will be my brothers forever. When we all meet up, it's going to be like New Edition and B2k getting back together.

To Malinda Carlson, I appreciate everything you have done for me these past five years of my life. I will always cherish our conversations we had at Illinois College.

To Illinois College, there will always be a special place in my heart for the beautiful school on the hilltop. I wouldn't change a single experience that I had in Jacksonville, Illinois. Thank you for changing me for the better.

Grambling State University, thank you for making me who I am today. You have given me all the tools that an HBCU provides for young African-Americans. GSU is a place "Where everybody is Somebody".

Special Thanks to:

Bobby and Kathy Conville

Jasmine and Lauren (Animation Team)

Cameron McDonald and Sabrina Hicks (Editors)

Everyone who answered surveys for me

D.N.

Jackson Parish Public Library

God I come to you humble than ever
You are the one who has gifted me with this skill
This is why I pray to you more than ever
You let me reach the people who need to hear my words the most
Yet, I struggle with the acceptance of failure that may come
Lord, you continue to bless me even when I get lost!
But you shine rays of light through me like I am the sun
I'm just the one who's trying to shed light amongst the sum
And when pressure seems to overcome me,
I pray and let you be the one who guides me
Lord when it comes to choosing soldiers you have millions to choose from
But you have given me the tools to use words that will make the pain numb
At 23 am I the one who should really let these people know
But what I have written in my heart, you will begin to show
And when I reflect back on how far I've came
I point at you and tell them God just told me stay in my lane
I come to you on my knees as a humble servant
Lord you tell me stand and continue to preach this sermon
I am the last one who should have but you never let me go without
Because I entrusted in you Lord, you never gave me a reason to doubt
And if I only have one crack at it, so be it
Just let the world always remember me for my kind spirit
Amen

Contents

Foreword- Malinda Carlson pg. 7

Momma I made it! pg. 20

First Day Out pg. 29

Wasted pg. 43

Real-ish pg. 56

It goes down in the Dm's pg. 71

Last Chance Who? pg. 80

Can I get fries with that? pg. 88

Me, Myself and Henny pg. 96

We learned what? pg. 105

#Adulting pg. 114

Foreword

How valuable is the college experience for individuals? Depending on the choices that are made, and the circumstances presented, these four to five years are tremendously significant in a person's life and defines who they are and determines in many ways which they will become.

If students attend college shortly after graduation and fully immerse themselves in college life such as sports or other activities outside the classroom, attend classes regularly, live on campus in a residence hall, and engage in thoughtful conversations with campus faculty, staff and students, these college experiences create different insights and new knowledge for individuals that create change or reinforce existing values and beliefs. It is probably unlikely that there will be another time in students' lives that so many changes will need to be navigated.

First-year students, newly on their own after graduating from high school need to adapt to a very different living space with either a stranger or someone that they do not know well. They will need to learn how to compromise, address conflict and increase communication skills to make this relationship work successfully, and as a result, they need to establish who their new group of friends will be and the behaviors and values that this group embraces. This decision has a profound impact on their college success.

Students also need to decide on their future career and what their major will be. This is challenging for most people. It is difficult for first-time students to choose what to eat for dinner any given night let alone to decide what profession they will have for the rest of their life.

Then there is the challenge of how to use the many hours of scheduled time during the day without parents, siblings and others structuring that time as has it been done previously for them. Knowing how much one must study for an exam, or how long it takes to research and write a paper, or how many times a document needs to be rewritten are all new experiences that need to be discovered and learned.

Even as an adult life after graduating from college, a person may experience a loss of employment, a divorce or a major illness, but usually a person's entire life is not uprooted as it is in the initial years of the college experience. Also, as people have more changes in their lives, they learn how, and they discover that these life challenges are relatively temporary and dissolve into new changes and challenges as each day of life unfolds.

With fifty years of experience working with students as they navigate the college experience, it is a pleasure to be asked to introduce a book written by a student with whom I got to know in his four years at Illinois College. As I reflect on the book he has written which I have not had the opportunity to read in its entirety, I take pleasure on commenting on my experience with this author, Joshua Hicks, and his journey at Illinois College and how this evolved in the successful person he has become. I also will also continue to elaborate on the challenges and choices that student's make and the impact that these decisions have. And I will finally conclude the introduction with some insights that I have gained as I have worked with the various generations of college students and finally, some of my guiding principles which have helped me and maybe will be of help to others as they maneuver life.

What helps students to become successful in college? To make this more personal, I will comment on the strengths that our author, Joshua Hicks, has which I believe contributed to his success at Illinois as well as his success after graduation.

Joshua was an out of state, Florida, a first-year student who arrived on a rural, small private campus knowing no one and needing to navigate a new culture and a new life on his own. What a challenge and what an opportunity! Sports were important to him, especially football, and so that initially created a base from which he would navigate the many other choices and experiences that he would have. Josh had many positives going for him such as a good family support system with great parents, a level of self-confidence that would serve him well, an extroverted personality, a willingness to take thoughtful and calculated risks, a willingness to learn and accept guidance and a care and respect for himself and others who were important in his life.

In addition to sports, Joshua chose to become involved in Literary Societies at Illinois College. Literary Societies are unique to Illinois College and to the Jacksonville community which is the home of Illinois College.

To provide a little background about literary societies, most present-day fraternities and sororities on college and university campuses began as literary societies. When college and universities started more expansive in the academic topics offered students, there became less of a need for students to pursue more liberal thought outside the classroom. Without that need to have more freedom for academic dialogue, literary groups became more social and evolved into our present-day fraternities and sororities.

Illinois College is unique in their maintaining literary societies with the opportunities for students to develop papers and present papers on the various topic to their peers. In addition, these Societies do provide a place where young men and women can support one another and develop a social network for friendships and social interactions.

I first met Joshua at the installation dinner for his class for the literary group, Pi Pi Rho. After a conversation at the table, and with a twinkle in his eye, Josh professed to me that I would be seeing more of him as the student leader for the group since he had goals and dreams for this new group that he had newly joined.

Joshua made more than good on this commitment. In a short time, I began to see t-shirts, sweatshirts, and other clothing articles and paraphernalia that reflected pride in the organization.

He organized his Society to do an outreach which validated the dignity of women and the respect that their group had for them. His Society did this by hand delivering stems of roses to all the women in all the other literary societies on campus. Pi Pi Rho also made it clear that any event held in their hall would reflect their respect for women and that their members would be accountable for any inappropriate or disrespectful behavior. This gesture was appreciated and well received by the women.

Josh also guided the group to have more conversations and interactions with faculty and staff on campus. Josh regularly visited me, and other members searched other faculty and staff on campus. The group began to make various faculty and staff honorary members and noted the recognition on Facebook and with special invitations to societal events.

The result of all these changes resulted in a tripling of membership for the group and a campus-wide recognition of the positive changes of Pi Pi Rho and the positive impact that Literary Societies can have on campus. Yes, one person can make a difference and in this case, that one person was Joshua Hicks.

College experiences have changed throughout the generations. In the fifties and early sixties, colleges were expected to be in 'loco parentis" or in other words, and we're supposed to assume the role of parent for the college student in the absence of the parent being on campus. So, during this era, colleges placed rules on students (more for protecting women than men) for visitation hours for the opposite sex in the residence halls, curfew hours, and dress codes for classes and dining facilities and the list goes on. In the late, the 60s and 70s, all of this changed.

Dress codes, visiting hours, and curfews were eliminated. Laws were put into place to protect student rights, and conditions were established regarding the sharing of students' personal information and conduct with parents and others. Students began to have choices and freedoms that were not availed to them in the past.

In the most recent years, the focus of higher education has been to make campus communities more welcoming and accepting of all minorities and diversity as it relates but not limited to culture, color, sexual preferences, and orientation, religion, political thought, some higher education institutions have been more successful in meeting this endeavor than others. Even though campus communities and students are more diverse than they ever have been, students continue to want to feel respected and valued for the talents, voices, and perspectives that they bring to the campus community.

When students arrive at college, I encourage them to commit to embracing the experience with an open mind and a willingness to listen and confidence to ask questions and have a voice. Students should not be hesitant or afraid to ask for clarity and to voice an opinion or feeling that they have. When opportunities arise, I will hope they dare to come forward and to lead in ways that are important to them. It takes courage, and it does come with risks, but that courage becomes more pronounced and more comfortable with practice. When students and campus officials work together at colleges, there can be real synergy and a sense of well-being, growth, and accomplishment for everyone involved.

As a professional in high education, I have tried, and I hope others in similar positions of influence in higher education might embrace the following tenants that are important to me. The first is that everyone has a story. When we truly listen to another person's story, we better understand that individual and realize that we have more in common than what we thought. We also have a better opportunity to help each other mutually. Secondly, what we do "in our corner of the world" makes a difference. Maybe we can't change the whole world, but we can define and influence those conditions and people that are closest to us. Thirdly, we need to role model and "act" on the way we want to be and should be. If we see or experience injustice, we are obligated not to complain about it, but, instead, to empower ourselves and others to address it most civilly and respectfully possible. Respect for one another and the ideas presented are critical to good communication, and good communication is essential for compromise, understanding, and acceptance. And, finally, change is a way of life. Conditions change around us continuously. People also change around us. And we, if we are growing and listening, should also embrace change. Yes, we all make our mistakes and misjudgments along the way, but hopefully, our changing involves learning about ourselves and the conditions of the world and result in our changing for the best. When we can be brave and confident to change, we open ourselves to embrace greater respect for ourselves, courage to be the best that we can be and confidence in helping others to be their best. Hopefully, by working together respectfully and embracing change, we can work toward a world filled with love, joy, and peace.

Momma, I Made It

Education must not simply teach work - it must teach Life. –
W.E.B. Du Bois

The day has come, your parents are smiling from ear to ear, and nobody tells you this yet, but your decision on what college to attend is the most significant decision in your young adult life. Prior to this, my only tough choice was what I should eat for lunch. I was an athlete in high school; the starting left guard for South Dade Senior High School. My senior year we won the Class 8A state championship, the first in school history. Fast forward to my signing day, for most kids it's filled with tv stations and ESPN has commentators pretty much foaming at the mouth to see where this top high school recruit will be signing his life …letter of intent to. Unfortunately, God blessed me with a lot of things, but height wasn't one of them. I signed my letter of intent to a division 3 school in Jacksonville, Illinois. A small Liberal Arts institution in Central Illinois, also known as J-Vegas. When it comes to making your college decision, you must understand that it is your decision to make. Your parents aren't the ones who have to attend class every day or practice (now, if your parents are the ones paying for school, I suggest you shut up and find an agreement on a place to call home for the next two-four years).

When deciding on where to attend college, you must focus on a few crucial criteria's; one is location. My mom always told me it's okay to go out of state for school, and the first opportunity I got I applied to schools all over, anywhere outside the state of Florida. You're reading, and you're probably saying, who wants to leave Florida, and Miami at that!? Florida is a tourist destination year-round. We have beaches, great weather, beautiful women, and some of the best party schools in the nation. Don't get me wrong, I love my home state, but attending college there was the farthest thing from my mind. I mean let's be real as an 18-year-old kid finally being on his own, there is no way I would've stayed on track in Florida.

Next, consider academics... no, I mean it. Most kids think a lot of their time won't be spent in a classroom, but you have no idea. Find a school with a field that you are interested in. As students, we all go into college with a set major in mind that we want to pursue, but in some cases, we end up completely switching. So, I suggest finding a school that has a couple of different programs that draw your interest. All schools are not created equally. This is the hardest part, deciding what type of institution will provide the best fit for you. You have state schools, and there are two kinds, anything that ends in "State University" rather than beginning with "University Of" is a party school for sure. Then, there's your Historically Black Colleges and Universities also known as HBCU's; you have Howard University, Florida A&M, Morehouse, and of course The Grambling State University which by the time you read this, will be my graduate school Alma Mater. Next, is your Liberal Arts and Private Schools. You will receive a top of the line education, but your pockets will feel every penny being taken away, it reminds you of Gollum in Lord of the Rings saying "precious"—every time you make a tuition payment. The best trend happening now, students attending a two-year community college and then transferring to a 4-year program to finish out. You save money and it is the ultimate G.P.A. booster, which helps you go from C's get degrees to Cum Laude quick.

Deciding on what school to attend can be a scary and strenuous process, and in all honesty, once you graduate from college, nobody even cares what school you went to unless it's an alumna of the college or someone who went to a rival school. My best advice is to choose a school that has apartment style dorms because if your freshman year was anything like mine you don't want to have a community bathroom. There's an old saying that there are more children in a community bathroom shower drain than in the world and if you don't get that reference believe me you will. Make sure to find a school that fits your personality; don't select a school just because your friends are attending that institution. Your happiness is the main thing that will get you through your time there. If you don't get accepted into your dream school, it's okay, attend another school that plays your dream school in football or basketball and cheer recklessly against them for not letting you in. I almost forgot an

IMPORTANT rule to remember when going to college. Dear freshman, PLEASE DO NOT BRING YOUR WHOLE ROOM WITH YOU!! It's annoying to walk into someone's room and they have stuff all over the place because they brought clothes from home that they wore in 7th grade and can't even fit. If you're going to school in South Florida here's a tip, you do not need any winter jackets so don't bring them. For all the ladies and guys who think they have the juice like a light skin rapper, don't bring all your clothes from your house because after the first week of classes nobody even pays attention to how you dress for class, especially if it's a morning class. I only say this because I was that freshman who brought everything I owned to college and let me tell you something, it is the biggest headache trying to pack all your stuff up at the end of the year and nobody is going to help you carry things down from the top floor of your dorm. Understand, once you go off to school things change and your schedule becomes a blur, but always take time out to call and check on your parents and family. In most cases, these are essentially the people who got you to this point and even though they want to be nosy sometimes, more importantly, they want to make sure you're safe.

Intermission

Realize that college will give you your best friends, the ones who will be in your wedding someday. Your friends will narrow down the older you get and don't worry your roommate you have freshman year, probably won't be your roommate the following year. You'll get homesick and think college might not be for you, I felt that way for about two days. You'll change your major, that's a guarantee. Heartbreak is in your future, it might not even be from an intimate relationship, but just someone close to you...that's life. You'll be put in situations that will make you ask yourself what type of person you want to be. Either way, you can no longer hide from the real world. Now that we got all the Pre-college talks out the way let's dive into what college is today. I want this book to serve as a guide that gives you all of college. In this book, I'll tell you the good, the bad and the nasty, but I promise to deliver the truth. This content will contain all the valuable information that a young student needs to know about college. None of that fabricated stuff your parents tell you, or what you have seen on television. I was fortunate enough to attend a Predominantly White Institution (P.W.I.) Illinois College, a community college for a summer (shout out Miami-Dade College), and I am currently enrolled at Grambling State University (HBCU) for my Master's. I'm no Stephen King, but some of these experiences might feel gruesome. This isn't Milk and Honey, but my relationship chapter might flow like Rupi

Kaur. This isn't Boy Meets world and I don't find my Topanga; this is College Uncensored. The untold stories that get left out of your college visit day or simply blacked out because the person informing you of college was under the influence. Life has its ups and downs, and nobody has the perfect college life, but that's what makes it fun. So, in the words of Lauryn Hill and The Fugees "Ready or not, here I come, you can't hide."

First Day Out

I did everything the streets told me was cool to do. Now I'd rather prove it to myself before I prove it to you. -Kodak Black

It's a hot Summer day in August—move-in day. The birds are chirping, All Gold Everything by Trinidad James is playing in the background, and Residential Assistants are wearing bright colored t-shirts. You pick up your room keys and head straight to decorating your room so you can show it off on Snapchat. Around now, your mom, or any woman that plays the motherly role in your life, has a smile on her face so wide you thought she went to Dr. Miami for a facelift. Now typically your dad, uncle or grandfather is the person who is moving your stuff into your room, so he probably has an attitude.

Like most freshmen, I was excited about everything college had to offer. You say to yourself: it's going to be just like the movies...you're going to make new friends, join a fraternity or sorority and pull every girl or guy on campus because you're the best thing on campus. First things first, take it easy young pup because Rome wasn't built in one day. Don't go in cocky like me, in most cases move-in day is a long tiring process. By the time you get into your room, set it up a hundred different ways, grab supplies/food from Walmart and do Freshman check-in, you will already need a shot of Jack. That was option number one for the eager new college student.

For my not-so-eager college students. The drive to your college campus will feel like the longest drive, you'll feel yourself getting farther away from home. You'll pull up to campus, and it will feel gloomy and the theme song of the day will feel like a sad commercial featuring Sarah Mclachlan. Many tears will be shed, and no matter how cozy they make your room feel, it may feel like you're serving a long prison sentence. Did I leave out you'll have a roommate? You see most colleges have you fill out roommate surveys before you move in and you have no control over who your roommate will be unless you're fortunate enough to attend school with someone you knew prior to college. Congratulations! Your roommate is now your significant other, and every decision that you make in your room must be mutual, or at least that is what your roommate agreement contract states that they make you sign. Despite everything that is going on the moment has finally come and you must tell your family goodbye, it's an emotional feeling that you can't explain, if you know then you know. When my parents closed my room door it felt like a scene straight out of Green Mile and Tom Hanks was walking me to my death. Moving in with someone you don't know is very uncomfortable because this person could possibly be crazy, nasty, a thief or all the above but in most cases, your freshman roommate is usually your first friend, and you two will be inseparable for the simple fact neither one of you know anyone else on campus. The best thing that got my mind off being away from home was one word... Coed or maybe it's two. Being in a building with girls is every man's dream, hell it's every woman's as well. Actor Jason Mitchell said it best "As a young guy you should never think the thoughts you have in your mind, aren't in a woman's mind" and in my mind, I was thinking straight sex. Now, I wasn't no John Tucker in high school, but in college, I could be whoever I wanted to be. I remember the wise words my father told me before I even left for college, he said: "now son, when you get to college do not fall in love with the first piece of p***y you get." I lived by that code and hell I didn't fall in love with the first girl I had sex with in college, but I did fall in love with the first girl who told me she loved me in college, but we can save that for a later chapter. Until you go to college, you never understand what freedom really is. College is the only place where you can stay up all night and nobody tells you to go to bed; you can eat whenever you want, skip class and be the most selfish person you want in life because it's just you taking care of yourself with no responsibilities besides going to class and or practice if you're in an extracurricular activity. All of this and more can be yours freshman if you get through orientation week or first-year students' week. Each school has a different name for it, and although at times it may get annoying, the different activities these schools put on for first-year students are helpful because you can get acclimated on campus and meet other new students who are just as lost as you. During this week they will have student organization sign-ups. If your high school was small or just didn't have many resources that you liked, don't worry college has it ALL. Fraternities and Sororities, chess club, Spectrum, Fellowship of Christian Athletes, debate, Black

Student Union, intramurals and Student Government. You name it they have it. College allows you to be the person you always wanted to be and then some. Take advantage of it and become actively involved, but don't bite off more than you can chew because you will find yourself overwhelmed. When it comes to Fraternities and Sororities, at this point, there are so many you can find one that perfectly fits you. It's not a cult, as weird as those sorority rush videos may seem, and fraternities just don't want you dying of alcohol poisoning, not going to lie that was messed up of me, but if you watch the news kids do crazy stuff to fit in. These organizations do a lot for the community within their area, well when it's mandatory. Black fraternities and sororities just aren't about stepping, it's not Stomp the Yard all day every day, but you will see them stroll a lot. Don't worry, either join or just watch from a far, but whatever you decide, just don't break their step line!! Joining a Greek Lettered

Organization allows you to be a part of something bigger than yourself. It's a brotherhood and sisterhood that you will be a part of the rest of your life. It's kind of like bad food, you can't run from it. If you thought college was going to be this special paradise where you got better food than in high school, you are sadly mistaken. The benefits of a college meal plan depending on where you attend vary. Most meal plans come with flex points where you can use these points in a campus convenience store or coffee shop. Some schools let you use your meal swipes for Taco Bell, Chick-fil-a, etc. It all just depends on how your school is set up, regardless don't eat the cafeteria food unless it's fried chicken day and if you don't attend a school in the south then you're SOL (Shit Outta Luck). I suggest you bypass the meal plan and save your money because the more you get adjusted to the college lifestyle, the more you will find yourself eating out. You can't beat the deals these restaurants, and fast food places give you. You have the "Becky with the good hair special" which involves a group of girls going to a Mexican restaurant for margs and queso dip. There are the "Y'all boys trying to chill? Special" which is usually a group of guys getting wings. One of my personal favorites "Do you take a student discount? special" which is probably any restaurant with a $5 box, $4for4, or a chicken special. Most importantly we can't forget the "I just got Paid special" which calls for an upscale type of restaurant such as sushi, Chili's, TGI Friday's whatever your heart desires, mine was Chinese. There's only one thing in college that will never ever leave your side, and that's Ramen noodles. This meal has been in more rooms than a campus security guard. I mean you can make it like a soup, or you can add toppings and make it a full meal, but whatever food path you go down just know "Freshman 15" is real, and it doesn't discriminate so just make sure to use your campus gym membership as well.

Timeout

Now, I want you to take a deep breath and just relax. I want you to be able to soak all these notes in like a sponge for my freshmen readers and for my readers who have already gone through the gauntlet, just reminisce and think about the days you were a nervous freshman. The day has come, and it's your first day of classes. For upperclassmen, it's hit or miss either you're happy because you got the professor you've been trying to register for a while and get or you're dreading it because you finally couldn't avoid the professor everyone has warned you about. When you're a freshman, you don't know what to expect. You want everything to be perfect from your outfit to your hair, to the smallest details of even getting the ideal seat. You're just hoping to see a familiar face from your dorm building or someone you met in freshman orientation, but as I said earlier take it easy, I'm here to look out for you. Depending on the school you attend, your classroom setup can go from a regular class to a computer lab to ultimately a lecture hall that can hold up to 200 plus students. Either way, every professor starts with a syllabus day or if the school is big enough, you get a whole week. Most large schools have TA's (Teacher Assistants) who run the class for the professor, if you become close with the TA (sleep with the TA) you'll pass the course, no I'm kidding... or am I? If you're more reserved and quiet, just show up to class and always ask questions. Most professors will give you a passing grade alone just for showing up and participating whether you know the answer or not. The benefits of attending a small college offers you the opportunity to build a bond with your professor and get that one on one attention necessary to help you be successful in class. Avoid sitting with a large group of your friends because none of you will be able to concentrate and will probably draw too much attention to yourself. Set up a class group message, not with too many people because the more people that are in it, the more likely you're going to get caught up. You set this group message up to help one another with homework, test, etc. College is nothing but a buddy system, even those kids you see with a 4.0-grade point average are probably using their Apple watches to cheat. The crazy thing is most professors know it's happening but are just too lazy to go through the academic protocol but if you ever run into a Professor whose name rhymes with Target Derrick good luck because that one eye Professor notices everything. I'm not influencing you to cheat, but I am influencing you to market yourself and use your resources around you. There will always be someone who knows more than you in a particular topic, so ask for help. These institutions take thousands of dollars from you, and you would be crazy to not take advantage of the campus speech center or writing center the school provides for you. Being a product of C's get degrees, trust me it's much cooler to make the Dean's list and academic all-conference.

Consummation

The hardest adjustment in college is your roommate situation. Some of you might be used to sharing a room with a sibling or a family member, but I promise college is much different. Regardless if you move in with your best friend since diapers, you will end up learning new things about them. You and your roommate can be complete opposites and want the room setup differently. Who gets the bed by the window, who gets the tv port, what's the rules on having guests in the room? All these questions will run through your head. If you're lucky enough and your dorm is set up like an apartment, each of you will have your own room and hopefully own bathroom. You will find out what type of person your roommate is just by the way they leave the bathroom. Not everyone grew up cleaning the bathroom on the weekends, some may take hour long showers... literally, and some can simply just be nasty. This can be an issue for you, but not to them. The best way to handle a situation is through communication, others might do more yelling than talking, but that's okay if you're getting out what needs to be said. I was fortunate to have the same roommate for three years. He and I just clicked; we never had any issues. We figured that if we simply communicated with one another things went a lot smoother. Sometimes I may have needed to study for an exam, so he understood that the lights in the room would be on longer than usual or one of us had a girl coming over and needed the place for a while, which is cool if you don't abuse the situation. Now if you happen to get a roommate who happens to start dating someone and that person is in your room more than their own, then hold a room meeting and talk to your roommate about it. They probably will get offended, but at least they know where you stand. If that doesn't work pull out that roommate agreement sheet that you signed at the beginning of the semester. Unfortunately, a percentage of you will get stuck with the one and done roommates. College is a tricky place, and if you're not mentally focused, you can get lost. Your roommate could struggle with being the life of the party and not focus on going to class which ultimately has them drop/fail out. Reality hits some, and it can be from family or financial reasonings. While others get to enjoy the miracle of life and have a baby. Regardless of the circumstance, you always remember your first roommate.

Wasted

Alcohol may be man's worst enemy, but the Bible says love your enemy. -Frank Sinatra

Ha, rock star lifestyle might don't make it

Living life high everyday click wasted

Sipping on purple stuff rolling up stanky

Wake up in the morning ten o'clock dranking

Party, party, party, let's all get wasted.

As the song Wasted by Gucci Mane plays in the back of my head, I can't help but think of the first college parties I attended. Being from Miami, I was used to house parties that usually ended with someone shooting up the party to let everyone know it was time to go. College, on the other hand, was a different breed. This might be the only thing that Hollywood and movies give an excellent portrayal of. College parties consist of alcohol, drugs, and half-dressed women; it's like living at Charlie Sheen's house. The whole point of a party in college is to make memories that you don't remember making and finding someone to hook up with, or at least that's how it felt. When it comes to parties, the atmosphere is different everywhere you go and mostly exclusive. Most big schools have bars and clubs that they attend like your college towns and if you're in a major city like Miami or Los Angeles good luck. Smaller schools rely on house parties thrown by someone on a sports team. Almost every school has Frat parties that are always lit because someone's trying to make it on "Do it for State." Which could be a good or a bad thing depending on the situation. Upon, coming to college, like most kids I never drank before. It's a personal choice that people must deal with on their own, either you're going to drink, or you're not. My exposure to alcohol came one night in a dorm room when a couple of my friends grabbed some Four Lokos. Tip #1 never start your first drinking experience with a Four Loko; it felt like I was drinking some syrup and I'm not talking lean either. Everyone has their go-to drinks when entering a party and depending on your mission for the night your beverage of choice can vary. If you're a beer drinker Natty Light will become your friend, because they give you 50 for only $8. Most girls love Uv or anything with a fruity taste. If you're a top-shelf connoisseur like myself get a bottle of Hennessy, I mean I did name a whole chapter after it. Either way you look at it, alcohol will be consumed. How much alcohol depends on how much you can take.

Don't get caught into the hype of "shotgunning, double fisting, and the most famous body shots." These are all quick attempts to get you trashed before the party even begins. Besides alcohol you have your drugs, I stayed clear of them but whatever floats your boat go ahead. There are so many different types of drugs nowadays who knows what's harmful and what's not. We're in the generation of Vapes and Juul pods, dab pens, whatever you want to call them. They're small and undetectable for the most part. Weed is your common drug, and nearly everyone does it or has tried it. Most drugs have all types of nicknames to appeal to the younger crowd but don't be surprised if you're taking a kind of ecstasy or LSD. Whatever you decide to do always be smart. Make sure that if you go to a party with your friends to turn on your location amongst your group message. Always travel in packs, my guys and I would walk into a party like we were in a scene of Goodfellas and nobody was going to break us up.

Interlude

There will always be college parties that you will remember for the rest of your life, some good, some bad. Either way, your life will be changed forever. As much as we give college parties their praise, I would be lying to you if I didn't bring up the harsh realities of what does and can happen in these settings. Let's address the elephant in the room; this interlude is about sexual assault. Like most teens entering college, I was nonchalant about the issue and quite frankly didn't think it happened as much as it did. If you're looking for statistics here they are according to the Huffington Post about 1 in 4 women will be sexually assaulted during their time at college. Not to make this bias by any means, I can give a personal story of how a situation can flip roles. One night a girl I was friends with texted me in the middle of the night, and like most guys I was hyped because I knew what opportunity was about to present itself. She let me know she was outside my dorm building and I went to let her in. By the time I opened the door she immediately hugged me, and I could smell the alcohol on her. At this point, I knew she was drunk, and she wanted to go up to my room, so many thoughts ran through my head as we walked up the stairs. For a whole semester, I wanted to have sex with this girl, and this was my chance. I knew the next day she would be sober and wouldn't remember anyway. This all felt too familiar, and I knew how this would play out. At the time I was a Black football player, and this was a sorority girl, who in mommy and daddy's eyes could do no wrong. So, I had the choice to either have one decent night with a girl who was more blasted than drunk uncle on a Saturday Night Live skit or deal with a rape charge. My inner ni**a came out, and I woke up my two best friends who stayed across the hall and told them we needed to get this girl home. I guess she became more incoherent between the time of her using the bathroom and me figuring a way to get her home because once she realized we weren't hooking up she started yelling at the top of her lungs and she stiffed armed me in the face. Screaming, f**k you! You don't want me anymore, and people were starting to wake up. Luckily for us, her girls came and got her and apologized to me about the scene she had caused". I know, not the story you were expecting huh? But the truth is most people aren't this lucky. Some guys take advantage of the situation and go through with it, traumatizing a woman for the rest of her life. Vice versa, sometimes a guy might be just as intoxicated and doesn't know what's going on and thinks he is just having a good time until he is being brought in front of a campus board for inappropriate conduct and his life is now in jeopardy. It's a hard subject to discuss between males and females because we will always have our own opinions on the situation. This is how I see it from a male's viewpoint. As a man, it is easy to be scrutinized by a group of individuals who see you taking advantage of a woman because in most cases we're bigger, stronger, and persistent as hell. We want to have a good time, and sometimes we fall into the pressure of our friends who might already have a girl for the night or may be misled with false information saying a girl is into you. It's not high school and these girls are now in their grown woman bodies and flirting all night with a drunk guy confuses us on the situation. I also know how the game is played and feel bad for women. If a girl is seen as a "hoe" or "thot" on campus, who is going to believe her when she says she's been sexually assaulted or raped? Most women must also live with the phrase "Boys will be boys" which is dumb because once you're in college we're all adults and a man should know the difference between yes and no. It's just not dealing with male classmates that these women must deal with, it's also men who are in higher authority that mentally rape these women with their eyes and try to be slick with it. It's a crazy world that we live in and we are letting our queens down. Well Josh, why won't these victims just come out and say they've been assaulted? Let's be real; it's the same reason why most people don't speak up about anything. When you're in a courtroom, a defense attorney's job is to make their client seem innocent. For a woman, her whole life is about to be exposed in front of a whole courtroom. Within minutes she will have to relive an entire incident that has traumatized her all over again. Then she will have to explain how many people she has slept with, how many people she has dated and if every individual gave consent each time they had sex. Let's hope for her sake that her body count is not in double digits because now the jury is thinking she's a hoe. The female victim is now emotionally torn and breaks down on the stand because her chances of winning this case are crumbling right in front of her.

One of my favorite shows that used to air on MTV was called "Sweet Vicious". It was about two female college friends fighting crime against campus sexual assault abusers on their campus. MTV states the show was canceled because of a lack of viewers, quite frankly I think it got the boot because it was too real for America and people just weren't ready to accept this real tragedy of what occurs on campuses daily. If you're a guy reading this, and you think I'm super feminist, Nah that's not the case. I'm just a man who holds his mother to the highest respect. Plus, if you really have "swag" like that with the ladies you can get her to say yes when she's sober too. I also acknowledge males whose lives have been tarnished because of false accusations. I know a few guys who have had sex with a woman and things didn't go her way, whether she wanted a relationship, or was just embarrassed that word got out that she had sex with a guy or group of guys. One of my homeboys got caught up in a rape case, not once did I ever believe he did it. You know a man's character, and you don't judge it! By the grace of God, he was found not guilty, but what it cost him will be in the back of his mind forever. If you know anyone or are a victim of sexual assault, contact this number (1-800-656-4673).

Last Act

I always refer to Michael Bennett because I'm currently reading his book and the guy just always knows what to say. In one of his chapters, he stated that he got involved in the woman's movement once he had his daughters. He understands that his job as a father is to protect his little girls and that he never realized how women should be treated fairly until he had to face the reality of his daughters coming across the same obstacles. Which in most cases I understand entirely, but who protects these young men when they get to college? Society has depicted all men as dogs, or at least my generation of men are written off that way. When it comes to rape or sexual assault we know it's about to be a woman giving a boring Ted talk about how "no means no." Throughout college my Head coaches made the team sign up for the #MeToo movement, and it was always dreadful because as a man you had to sit in a room for an hour and hear how evil men were. As a freshman, you laugh, and you say what type of person puts themselves in this situation? But as you get older and grow closer to girls on campus, they begin to talk about an incident that they or a friend has been through. You never know what truly happens behind closed doors, but for my male readers be smart. Don't let a little liquid courage be the reason for making a mistake that you'll regret in the long run. You might be wasted just like them, and this might be the only opportunity you get to have where it's just you and them. They're in front of you asking for it and, at that moment, you must decide. Do you be mature about the situation, or do you embrace the situation and have your way. Those few minutes of power you have with that person does it depict who you truly are?

Real-ish

I feel like I lack a lil' knowledge

I know I'll never make it to a campus of a college.

We were the ones that used to pick on the scholars. -Mozzy

(Interlude)

I wish I could tell you that college was perfect, but it wasn't. Unlike high school, you can no longer hide yourself from the real world. You are bound to meet new people from a different background, race, religion and even sexuality. For me, I went from a diverse city and a high school that was practically a melting pot to a college that was Black and White. I had no idea what I was getting myself into choosing a school located in Illinois. One of my first memories at Illinois College was when they separated my freshman seminar class up, and all the Black students ended up in the same room. I didn't think much of it then, but now looking back they probably did it on purpose. Both of my parents graduated from Grambling State University, a Historically Black College and University located in Louisiana. So, telling my parents, I would be attending a majority Institution was a big step. They couldn't prepare me for what was going to happen next because they never experienced a PWI on the college level. Like being a Black man in the United States wasn't hard enough. I remember holding a conversation with a girl in my class, and she made this remark: "You're not what I expected" Me being so clueless I had no idea what she meant, so I told her to elaborate. She continued by saying "You know? You're not like how they act on television". If I told you I was shocked that would be an understatement. I was more disappointed in the fact that it was 2014 and I was her first Black interaction. I could've cursed her out, but by doing that, I would have just been that angry Black man she had seen on television. Illinois College taught me a lot about myself in four years that it would've taken almost a lifetime to understand. Even now I would not trade my experiences for the world. IC gave me the motivation to dig deeper into the college lifestyle, and I wanted to see both sides of the college system.

By the time you read this, I would have probably received my Master's degree from Grambling State University. That's right after undergrad; I needed to see how the other side was and get my "Wakanda" on with my HBCU family. There are so many differences from a PWI and an HBCU; both have their pros and cons. At a PWI there are hardly any long lines whatsoever, but at Grambling, you better pack a snack because you'll be waiting all day. Everyone speaks at Grambling when walking pass each other, but at IC we could make eye contact and people would still walk right pass me. There are always similarities though because at the end of the day we're all college kids just trying to figure out who we are. I think Drake said it best "I'm here for a good time, not a long time."

Intermission

The harsh reality of college is this, for most young adults you have been taught what to say and how to think for 18 years of your life. When you finally come to college your brain is all over the place. You can be a kid from Montana who has never been around a person of color and it scares you. The preacher's kid who gets paired with the gay kid from a city who embraces all walks of life now must figure out how they will get along because his religion states it is morally wrong to think this way. Finally, you have the privileged kid who has never had to work a hard day in his or her life rooming with an illegal immigrant whose parents worked endlessly in the fields to save enough money to help their child chase the American dream. This is when you scream "This is America!". Nah, I'm kidding "This is college" and believe it or not students deal with this reality every day. This chapter is dedicated to the voiceless, the students who may be afraid to let you know college is not all sunshine. The crazy thing about college is everyone has their assumptions about one another. If you're a minority at a majority White institution, you believe you have it rough, if you're in the LGBTQ+ community every day is a constant battle because people hate different and if you're White your fellow minority peers think you're one-sided as far as politics go. Unfortunately, we live in the era where social injustice seems to be okay. NFL superstar and overall activist Michael Bennett speaks about intersectionality in his book, "Things that make White People Uncomfortable" I know the book title might be off-putting to some, but then again you might be the person who he refers to as being uncomfortable. What you must understand when it comes to college is that everyone wants their voice to be heard, but which crowd are you trying to reach is the question you must ask yourself. Currently on a college campus somewhere you have Black Student Union fighting for the Black Lives Matter movement, Latino Student Union fighting against the deportation of immigrants across the country and Trump supporters screaming make America great again! Which the only time America was great was when gas prices were below $2. Don't worry LGBTQ+ community I didn't forget about you or the constant struggle that you go through. The issue that I have is all organizations have this crab in the barrel mentality and what I'm referring to is when you put a bunch of crabs in a bucket they climb all over each other just to reach the top and can care less who gets hurt. Once you step foot onto campus, you are ambushed by a group of upperclassmen who lowkey profile you before you even walk to their table. I had Black Student Union all over me before I could even make eye contact, do you really think someone from the Japanese club would approach me? Which is funny because I did sign up for the Japanese club in undergrad. That fraternity or sorority that you were thinking of joining already scouted you out before you put your name on that interest paper and in most cases, they already decided if they wanted you. I can only relate to Black students on how it feels to be a minority on campus, and I did my senior thesis on how it is to be Black at a majority institution. Here are some Quotes that I received from my research on Black students attending a PWI:

"I feel that if people didn't know how good I was in a sport or campus organizations, my white peers wouldn't talk to me and vice versa."

"I wouldn't go to anyone on campus because I don't think they care personally; they are just there to be a listening ear and know your business. I don't think they'll give me what I need; they'll probably be afraid to say something because it might come out the wrong way."

"You can count on your fingers the number of Black people on campus like there's not that many. I don't think Black voices are heard or respected on campus, and I feel like we're listened to enough to shut us up. Like they make us feel like they heard us, but they haven't and, they give us that little piece that makes us quiet."

This is just one side of how college is for a minority student but be real with yourself if you're a minority your whole life has been unbalanced. Referring to oneself as a minority doesn't have to be strictly based on race, let's flip it and discuss being a member of the LGBTQ+ community. During my junior year due to random selection and an open spot in our room, my roommate and I were paired with a gay guy. I have no issue with anyone who happens to be homosexual, but this guy was 6 foot 3 and was built like a linebacker from Alabama and just so happen to be Beyoncé's biggest fan. If you could take a participant from RuPaul's drag race, he would be the perfect image. At first, it was embarrassing to tell people that this was my suitemate, but that was merely just my ignorance and lack of maturity kicking in. Not once did I ever think of how he felt living in a dorm with two football players. This guy put a smile on his face everywhere he went just to be looked at like he was an animal in a new zoo exhibit. He was never afraid to let people know that he was proud to be who he was. I admired that about him because he showed me that people will always talk, but it's up to you on what you give them to talk about. Just sitting down talking to him one day he told me this "College is a constant struggle for everyone. It's hard being a minority in America, but imagine how hard it is to be a gay Black man in America." I never thought about it like that before, but he was right. If he had to live life with a double-edged sword with the words "hate" going across it who was I to complain. When it comes to ethnicity Latino/Hispanic students must go to school in worry every day in fear of being deported. To not only be in worry that you have a final to pass but that "ICE" can come in at any time and arrest you is quite frankly bullshit. There was a girl back in undergrad who spoke in a showcase, and she told us how she spent her winter break in a holding prison. She wasn't illegal, but her parents were, and they finally released her. The crazy thing is I think she mentioned how she was a triple major and was graduating with some of the highest honors, yet we want to deport a woman who could probably run a Fortune 500 company. For my White readers, your college experience will honestly be what you make of it. But when it comes to "real-ish," it will be hard. Don't be afraid to voice your opinion on campus, it's your school as well, but be open and hear your peer's views too. Just because you watched the movie Black Panther doesn't mean you're down for the movement, but we appreciate the effort and understanding for you finally being "woke". Regardless of the color of your skin, financial background, religion or sexual orientation, always remember the word "RESPECT" because you'll never know when it can be you on the outside looking in.

Outro

August 12, 2017 was the day of the Charlottesville riots, which left one woman dead and 19 injured. The night before a fight had broken out on the University of Virginia campus because emotions were running high over the removal of the city's

Confederate past. To refresh your memory some more, September 2015 the University of Missouri, Columbia had racial issues on campus which ultimately ended with the resignation of the school president. I mention these two incidents because racial tension is alive and well on college campuses. They're in your classrooms, your dorms, your frat houses and in most cases right in front of your face. Every year there are reports of fraternities making pledges do crazy things, but Theta Tau of Syracuse had pledges perform a skit using racial slurs. It's 2019, and we are still having the same problems. This isn't a Black and White thing; this is everyone's problem. I went to watch the movie BlacKkKlansman with my parents, and the background of the film is about an undercover Black cop in Colorado pretending to be a member of the KKK. Spike Lee and Jordan Peele killed it as usual with the visual effects and deep moral meanings behind everything. What stuck out to me was this older White woman approaching my mother in the bathroom and apologizing because she felt embarrassed of how White people had treated Blacks so poorly. She continued saying how the movie touched on all bases and hatred in America is a serious problem. She stated her son is gay, and she knew how people could be ignorant and insensitive. I wondered to myself and thought of how many people felt this way. This sense of discomfort, yet nobody says anything. An old classmate of mine blamed her hometown because there were no other minorities and she wasn't taught how to interact with people of different racial backgrounds, so college was a cultural shock. In undergrad, we had this room called the diversity center designated for everyone on campus, but only the Black and other minority students took advantage of the space during my first two years there. When asking my White peers why they never went inside they usually just shrugged their shoulders and let their facial expressions do all the talking like "I'm White, I can't go in there." That defeated the purpose of calling it the "Diversity Center" because it's for everyone. We allow ourselves to be trapped in this bubble of what space is for who. I learned that in the mountains of Boone, North Carolina where Appalachian State University is located that minority students play a significant role in how the school is ran. That App State is a big politically active campus, and more colleges need to take note. We must get comfortable with talking about these topics. I have no idea if they already have committees like this, but each college campus needs a diversity panel made up of students from different races, nationalities, sexuality and political parties, which meet with the campus board monthly and discuss issues on campus to make their school a safe zone for everyone. As my generation gets older, the more I realize we don't stand for anything unless it has a hashtag in front of it. We'll protest for one day and post on social media, yet we don't follow up. The school President might suspend or terminate someone, and we think the job is done, but we fail to realize that the battle has just begun. It's bigger than ourselves, we owe it to the people who fought and marched before us, we owe it to the future, and quite frankly we owe it to ourselves!

It Goes Down in the DM's

I love the 'Gram, I love the 'Gram

I'm addicted to it, I know I am. -Yo Gotti, (Down in the Dm's)

Back when your parents went to college they probably gave you all these romance stories of how they first met, and how it was love at first sight. This might be a shocker to some, but that's not how college works nowadays. Everything today revolves around social media. Hint why the chapter is called "It Goes Down in the DM's," it's rare that when you see a guy or girl for the first time on campus that it's your first time seeing them. Somehow the universe has had you run across this person's page on Instagram, or you've seen them on a mutual friends Snapchat story, but the likelihood that it's your first time seeing them is slim to none. Our social skills as a generation suck, the fact that most guys can sit right next to their crush in class and not say a word is mind-blowing but will be the first person ten minutes removed from class in her DM's saying "You tryin' to chill? For my female readers, you will receive more direct messages from guys in your four years than campus announcement emails. Don't worry guys because women slide in the DM's too, but they more so set us up with the thirst traps on their Instagram account to lure us in. Women say how much they wish a guy would approach them in person and talk to them. But let's be real ladies if you're with your girls and a guy approaches you, and he's not up to your "standards" you're going to show out in front of your friends and give this poor dude the biggest L of his life. One of my best friends always referred to women as an NBA2k video game, in which you must think like Steph Curry and keep shooting your shot until eventually, one falls in. The best way I could explain a college relationship is kind of like an Amazon

Prime membership; you love it until the free trial ends. Dating in college is a lot like that except your free trial ends after six months. It usually begins with adding each other on social media or through a mutual friend. Snapchat is your best friend ladies and gents because it's the ultimate ice breaker. You can hold conversations with one another, and the message deletes right away unless you run into a girl who likes to save the messages and use countless amounts of filters, which at that moment guys you have a tough decision to make on how to approach her from there. For my female readers, life is easy for you. If you're not into a guy or you don't trust him, give him the snap and decide later if you want to unfollow him. Being in a relationship during college is split into three stages. Stage one is the "talking" period which is the most famous stage because everyone claims they're talking to someone and usually the other person has no idea that they're in that stage. It typically requires you two snapping and texting each other throughout the day, which is a big deal for our generation because if you find someone who can hold an actual conversation long enough to be entertained, they might be the one. Stage two is the "public appearance" stage which includes no longer inviting that person over to your room during the "on dirt" periods of the day such as noon, 10 pm, or any time after midnight hours. Taking pictures after a game or at a party and posting it on your social media are all accessories to the public appearance stage. Finally, around month three you reach the final stage where it is Facebook official, and all your friends say, "it's about time." For most college relationships if you make it past six months you are doing well and might be in love, but then that free trial runs out, and it's time to move on to the next person.

Interval

Trust is something that you can only earn. Social media might be one of the greatest entertainment inventions to humanity, but it has single-handedly ruined relationships for our generation. Don't like this person's picture or don't get a streak with this person on Snapchat because someone might get jealous. Of course, you might say, if you trust your boyfriend or girlfriend you shouldn't even worry about that. Which is true but trust only goes so far before paranoia starts getting the best of you. College is a place where you can hook up with as many people you want without being judged... if you're a guy. It's all about reputations, and unfortunately, women don't get the same opportunity. If you're a freshman girl and enter college with a body count of one guy and leave your freshman year with a body count of two, rumors can spread and say you slept with everyone because of the one guy you hooked up with or dated, because he told everyone. It's not right, but it happens. Unfortunately for that girl who did let loose her freshman year, she now must deal with everyone in her inbox, and she continues to get hurt because she's trying to find Mr. Right. The crazy thing is, just like in high school the good guy finishes last again because no girl wants the nice dude. You're in the friend zone the night you decide to be her shoulder to cry on. NBA superstar Iman Shumpert said it best "No girl wants a guy who walks into the party and gets no love from other women. Every woman wants the man who walks into the building, and a woman goes out of her way to get a hug from him" because that dude is respected regardless of his relationship track record. Our values get lost because it's more important to us on how many likes we receive next to the person we're standing with rather than the person who truly satisfies our needs emotionally, mentally and physically. I worry about this all the time. I'm in my early 20's, and this Drake line plays in the back of my head repeatedly "I feel like I'm bound to be with somebody that's been with everybody." Who knows maybe college damaged me relationship wise. Perhaps it's the craziness I witnessed my boys go through with their girlfriends or karma might be having its go with me for playing with a couple girls' hearts during undergrad because I thought I was the man. I'm not saying you can't fall in love in college and find your spouse because there have been plenty of people I know who are genuinely happy, but I know a few still trying to pick up the pieces from prior relationships as well.

Epilogue

Being young, we have this messed up entitlement that love is going to play out the way we want it to. We live in this world nowadays where it's more acceptable to have a kid, but not even be married to the baby's mother and have no intent on marrying her either. Which is cool, I understand things happen, and you had no idea that your partner was not compatible until a baby came into the mix. Or maybe it's because we're still kids ourselves. During your college years, you can throw out this four-letter word like it's nothing because everyone has their meaning behind the word love. Around my sophomore year of undergrad, I found myself in love with this one girl. I had gotten myself so wrapped up in the thought of being in love, that I didn't even understand her definition of love was different than mine. Yeah, it ended with some shots of Hennessey with Drake playing in the background, but I'll save that story for a little bit later. College is a mental rollercoaster filled with emotions, and you must deal with everyone from the outside world chiming in on your relationship. Handling people breaking all types of bro and girl codes just because they secretly want your relationship to end. The people who post their relationships the most on social media are the ones usually with the most problems, because nobody cares that you two had a fun time at IHOP, because we all assumed you two had fun anytime you were together, so who are you trying to convince? We all want this love that can be seen in movies. The question is, who's willing to let their guard down first? As horrible as this analogy is if you ever saw the show One Tree Hill, one of the main characters named Peyton always refers to people leaving. That no matter how much you care for someone, that they will still go. Sometimes we anticipate the worse and forget to savor the moments that leave us with a smile because for every heartbreak there was a heart first…

Last Chance Who?

Why should we have to go to class if we came here to play FOOTBALL, we ain't come to play SCHOOL classes are POINTLESS. -Cardale Jones

Dear NCAA athlete,

This one is for you...

For some of you, the life of being a collegiate athlete has always been your lifelong dream. It's a glamorous lifestyle, to say the least. If you're lucky enough to be recruited by a big-time college program, your life is going to change drastically. Let's be honest, that same recruiter who always called and texted you in high school, no longer checks in on you because their job was to get you to the school, and they did that. The same coach that sat in your living room telling mom or grandma that you're their number one priority and that they'll treat you like one of their own kids is the same coach screaming at you saying why'd they give you a scholarship. You don't go to school to be a student; you go to college to be an athlete. Most of your days are centered around your sport, and you usually take the 9 or 12 credit hours it takes to be considered a full-time student, but you'll realize that the area that you wanted to major in doesn't work around your athletic schedule. Which means your academic advisor is about to put you in a major that you didn't even know existed. College is a business. If you're eligible, that means the team wins and if the team wins the school makes money. All at the task of you receiving a degree in Animal/Livestock Husbandry Production (No offense to anyone who majored in that field), but your advisor will make you major in something like that knowing damn well you're from Los Angeles and never been around a farm animal a day in your life. But the department chair is a huge athletic fan, so it's cool. Don't worry because you'll forget about that momentarily when it's Christmas in August. That is how your average athlete refers to getting new gear from the schools' apparel sponsor. If you went to a poor public high school like me, then you would think receiving free gear from Nike or Adidas was compensation. That's just a cover-up for what they really owe you. As an athlete you're on tv quite a bit and depending on where you attend school, little kids wish to be in your exact shoes wanting to imitate everything you do. So, if you wear two Nike sleeves, you can guarantee a kid from your old neighborhood is watching and wants their parents to buy two Nike sleeves for them. My dad and I always debated over whether college athletes should get paid, but to be honest, it's a tricky situation. The star football player at Alabama is not struggling because boosters are making sure he's getting fed, but what about that 4th string running back who is barely on the team? Who is helping feed this kid? Because sometimes people have personal things at home that need to be taken care of and that free meal plan isn't paying the bills at mom and pops house. The University of North Carolina's football team had gotten in trouble for players selling their team shoes. Which is mind-blowing to me because everyone in the NCAA gives away team gear to friends and family, but the NCAA must find a way to get involved in taking someone's money if they're not getting a percentage of it. Urban Meyer who was the Ohio State Head football coach was set to make $7.6 million in 2018, yet he was given a paid leave of absence for a couple games, because his assistant coach was beating his ex-wife and Meyer had seemed to have known about it. (Which reminds me of being in a team meeting one day and my coach said, "You're guilty until proven innocent" what a guy... I'd never call him if I got in trouble.) Former UCF football player Donald De La Haye lost his scholarship due to him making

YouTube videos and getting paid. Which still puzzles me a little because the Cleveland Browns signed a player, who was also a rising music producer who produced songs for Rick Ross and DJ Khaled during his time in school. He proved that an athlete does not have to put themselves in a box. I could've sworn college was supposed to teach us how to make a living for ourselves and influence young adults to want to go in business for themselves. Two college kids just trying to make a living for themselves. I guess the only way a student-athlete can make money is either taking money under the table or wait for a refund check.

Halftime

Last Chance U is this documentary series on Netflix that follows the lives of Division 1 football players who attend a junior college, typically in the middle of nowhere, trying to get a second opportunity at life. It gets you sucked into the lives of these athletes and their struggles, and by the end of the season, all you want to do is see them succeed. When it comes to being a collegiate athlete, the most underappreciated division is of course Division 3. Being a D3 product I can tell you nobody has it worse than us. Long bus rides, high school equipment and pretty much paying to play the desired sport you love while being on the same type of schedule as a power five Division 1 athlete is hard. If you don't understand the rules and how lopsided college athletes are treated, I'll break it down. A power 5 FBS (Football Bowl Subdivision) like your Alabama's and LSU's can give 85 scholarships on its roster. Your FCS (Football Championship Subdivision) like North Dakota State can give away 63 scholarships with 30 players able to get aid. Then you have Division 2 programs such as Northwest Missouri State, who can give away 36 scholarships. Then there are your Division 3 programs such as Illinois College, who can give away 0 athletic scholarships. Even NAIA and Juco's can give out athletic scholarships. During my time playing, we received $9 per diem when coming back from a football game. To tell you how crazy it really was, our coaching staff would typically let us eat in the food court of a mall and if you ever ate in a mall food court their prices are a little bit under what you would pay for at a professional sporting event which means your $9 isn't getting you a thing. One time I was a few cents short for my meal, and my assistant coach was struggling too, so he couldn't even help make up the difference. So, when players who have full scholarships do ridiculous stuff like steal or get arrested, the selfish side of me feels upset because I was struggling while these Division 1 athletes got special treatment. Maybe my struggle as a D3 athlete help teach life lessons that I was too naïve to understand at that moment. Jameis Winston is a quarterback for the Tampa Bay Buccaneers and was always in and out of trouble when he was at FSU. The book was never thrown at him because he was a star athlete, and after a while, you tend to build this powerful feeling about yourself that nothing can harm you. When he was the one hurting himself all along. Well, that's what the media will report, nobody wants to blame the NCAA, NFL or FSU for always bailing him out. This is when a bad reputation for all college athletes is built. Regular college students lowkey hate student-athletes because they think all athletes are self-absorbed booster money abusers. Students think athletes get a free pass in classes which in some instances are true. Regular students think athletes get whatever they want which again in some cases are true as well. We can't leave out that most women think all male athletes are players which is partially true, but it comes with the territory. All these points have valid reasons for a student to feel some way towards an athlete; but before you write all athletes off, place yourself in their shoes. At 5 A.M. when you're asleep in your bed, these athletes are getting ready for practice or morning lifts. All those pre-game parties and tailgates you get drunk at, are because you're going to watch those athletes play. When you get to go home for a holiday break, these are the same men and women sacrificing their family time to represent your school. But they get full scholarships, so it pays off right? Wrong. When you must carry the burden that most of these athletes have on their back, you'll be wishing to switch places back. I understand, some athletes drive around in Camaros on campus, and you wonder how someone straight out of the inner city could afford it. Don't worry I have those same thoughts too, but maybe that car is just a little bit of what the school owes these athletes after making millions off of them.

Overtime

The number one goal to obtain while being a college athlete or a student, in general, is to graduate. If someone is willing to give you a full scholarship why not use them like they're using you. It doesn't even matter what you get your degree in as long as you walk across that stage and receive that piece of paper. Your sport is temporary, and I don't have to breakdown the odds of someone's chances of making it professionally. If you hate school, find something that's going to get you through. Avoid being another statistic of a hometown hero who went off to college but couldn't make it pro and now is struggling to get a decent job because they never received their degree. Those people aren't bad people, but I know they would go back in time if they could. Take a business class and learn how to invest your money, that way you'll always be good regardless if you make it to the league or not. Education is the key to the future.

Can I Get Fries with That?

Used to pray them Ramen noodles turned into Lobster. -Meek Mill (We Ball)

If you think you know struggle go off to college. College is the only place where you can pay for a meal plan and still be hungry. The biggest mafia in America is the collegiate system. If you're wondering why I refer to them in that way, miss one payment and see what happens. Every institution handles the issue differently. Some schools call and send mass emails to get your attention. If you attend an HBCU, they're dropping you from the class no questions asked, play with them if you want too. You get charged for everything regardless if they hide it in your tuition payments or make you pay for it separately. Parking decals, student ID's, even scantrons are all fees coming out of your pocket. Hell, you spent money just to apply to a school that you weren't guaranteed to get accepted into. Once you get established on campus, you find out that this food catering company sponsors your school. If an upscale private catering corporation sponsors your school cancel your meal plan. Since we're in the age of lawsuits, I can't directly name the company, but you know who I'm referring to. Supposedly there are different levels of this fine dining, but if you're not attending an Ivy league school, the meals are probably all equal to garbage. You gain your "freshman 15" by always eating out and trying to avoid the cafeteria. Besides spending money on food, being in college, you spend half of your money on alcohol or drugs. Learn the system and divide your cash if you're buying alcohol settle for the cheap brands. Yeah, the taste can vary anywhere from piss water to rubbing alcohol, but if you paid $5 for a haircut would you really expect it to be great? The same rules apply for alcohol. All your financial experiences will provide life lessons that you and your friends will laugh about in the years to come. Deciding whether to put the whole $20 in your gas tank or dividing it into $5 for the night so that you can have $5 in the tank, $5 for alcohol, $5 for the party and $5 for a late-night McDonald's or Taco Bell run after the party, will have you think you're a genius but, you're just buying time. I love all my accounting majors, but I think every kid who leaves college should have the basic grasp of accounting skills because nobody can stretch a dollar better than a college kid besides your single mothers and crackheads, but they're excluded from this point I'm trying to make. It's hard to go on a date nowadays because you can quickly drop $30-$40 dollars just on the movies alone. Guys don't be ashamed to abuse that student discount. Be creative! Your date will be happy regardless. I'm telling on myself, but my favorite thing that I used to do was rent a kid's movie from Family Video, like the Lion King because it was free and then I would order food from the local Chinese restaurant at 3 because it was still lunch prices and just warmed it up later; best spent $10. Ladies don't judge me; I was trying to work with what I had. Just understand college is a partnership and we're struggling together, so don't be afraid to help spend some money on the date either ladies.

Spring Break

It doesn't matter when you go or where you go; each college student needs to experience Spring break. It's the only time in your life where being drunk 24/7 is acceptable. You have Miami, PCB, Fort Lauderdale, Destin, Daytona, Cancun, and South Padre are a few options on the list that you can decide from. My crew had the opportunity to experience Fort Lauderdale, Florida.

For all my readers who attend school in Kentucky... Thank you!! Because you all know how to party. I now understand why Drake said "I need a girl from Kentucky" it all makes sense now. The state of Kentucky is hiding some beautiful women from the rest of the country. This section will be rather short for the simple fact that I don't remember much from the trip. You will spend most of your time on the beach, meeting new people from different schools and exciting fights amongst drunks. Make sure to get enough hotel rooms. That old folk tale about not really being in your room that much is false because once you have been in the sun all day and drinking the last thing you want to do is share a bed with two other people. Spring Break flings are real as well. Doesn't always mean something sexual is going to happen; it can just mean you meet someone you click with and talk to during the break.

Double Shift

If you're lucky, you will never have to work a job during college, but for most students that luxury is not an option. Most institutions have job fairs during welcome week, where students have the option of working on campus or off. If you're like me, you're trying to work in the office so that no matter what happens you get to see every female on campus. I was able to work for the Dean of students during undergrad, and it was easy money. If you decide to work on campus, the downfall, is you get paid once a week or month. You're making minimum wage which will only give you enough pocket money. Most students decide to work off campus, and I have respect for these students because they have it tough. They're easily behind student-athletes for having a tough college experience as far as trying to have excellent time management skills. Often, these students get overlooked for their dedication to being a student and worker because society assumes that once you hit college that you should be able to multitask, but honestly, it's stressful going to work, having class and then being expected to study for a test and get the essential six-eight hours of sleep recommended. To my readers who are working those double shifts while being a full-time student, salute to you all. Finally, can't leave out the students who are also full-time parents. You all are the epitome of great examples. The hours that you all put in easily go unnoticed, and it doesn't matter how old you are because you are trying to better your life as well as your family's life. By the time graduation comes along the average student will be in debt and our excellent student loan companies are so thoughtful because they give you six months to prepare to pay them back... I had classmates who didn't even know what they wanted to do with their lives after graduation, so how could someone possibly assume six months is enough time for a person to get their life together. What exactly are we paying for? Guess we can try to figure out the answer to that question together in chapter nine.

Me, Myself and Henny

The Same thing that makes you laugh, can make you cry. -Sly and the Family Stone

I've personally been waiting to get to this chapter. Chapter 8 is personal just for the simple fact it's about me. There are no rules or tips to follow, and it's just me speaking on my college experience. Being in Jacksonville, Illinois wasn't a cultural shock as much as a gut check. It could be tied to the same feeling as waiting for your professor to post the final exam grade, you have a feeling of what it is, but your stomach is in knots trying to see what the outcome will be once it's posted. Being a thousand miles away from home, I needed to find myself. No longer did I have to report to anyone but myself. For the first time in my life, I wasn't worried about school or my grades; I was soaking up everything college threw at me. Juggling classes, football, and a social life were hard at first, but my parents instilled in me from an early age on how to have time management. I wish those were the only obstacles I had to face, but unfortunately, it wasn't. Entering college, I was no longer considered a boy, and I guess the rest of the world saw that as well. I was now considered an adult Black man, which in some people's eyes makes me viewed dangerous, or that's what people's perceptions were. Jacksonville, Illinois made that clear. Walking into Walmart and everyone was looking at you like you might steal something gets old. I live in Louisiana currently, and the White people here don't even look at me like that. Being treated like a second-class citizen at Applebee's was an experience in itself. They were better off telling my friends and me to come through the back door as they did during the Civil Rights Era. Being on campus was no better at times. Dealing with some professors who paid attention to you taking a test rather than the other 15 non-Black students who were cheating off one another was crazy. Most people would ask "Why not report the issue?" Maybe, it was the ignorance of the G code that "you don't snitch" or that nobody would believe us… damn, maybe that's why nobody reports sexual assault. I had one professor who probably stayed up all night trying to figure out how to fail my friends and I rather than just doing her job. Honestly, I want to thank that professor because she taught me that no matter how many degrees you have, it still can't buy class. During my time in undergrad, I was fortunate enough to be the first Black President of my Literary Society or at least nobody has evidence of another one prior to me. As President, I was able to construct the largest pledge class in society history along with my Pledge educator Quinn Allen. Many hours were put into it, and once my Presidency was complete, our membership had tripled. I was passed over on being a trustee which bothered me for a while because I knew if I looked like my other peers that would have never happened. With trials and tribulations, I was able to make the best out of my situation, and it was honestly the best move for me at that point in my life. In the Spring semester of my freshman year, I was able to meet some of my best friends, but they turned into my brothers. We all were from out of state, minorities and played football. Our connection was instantaneous. They each taught me something different about myself that I didn't think I had in myself. Tyree taught me how to be vocal. Always telling me if I didn't agree with something that I should speak up and that moment came during our senior year in a football meeting when our Head coach brought up the Colin Kaepernick situation. At that moment I didn't know what came over me, but I couldn't agree with my coach on this certain topic because it was bullshit. The Black athletes always spoke in private, but we never voiced our opinions on issues, and I was tired of being silent. I don't know if my point got across, but I earned the respect of my teammates that night. Next, is my boy Greg from Alton, Illinois. He is the comedian of the group, and he taught me how not to have a filter. Until this day I say what I mean and mean what I say. Dakotah lit the fire for my militant side. He will debate you about anything, and if you don't have your facts right, he was going to eat you alive. Michael was my roommate for three years. He was the quiet one of the group, but if there was a picture next to the word loyalty in the dictionary, it would have Mike's face by it. Loyalty was always key to me, and Michael always reminded me of it. Then there's Josh, and yes, we share the same first name. Josh taught me how to live in the moment. Forget tomorrow because it's not promised. All we have is right now, so why not make the best of it. To the woman, I was able to meet during my time at IC and having the pleasure of loving, you gave me the vision to dream big. You showed me the beauty of all the imperfections the world had to offer because people like you and I were put here to make a difference. Love isn't just an emotion; it's a lesson. Our last two years of school ended in more arguments than it did happy memories, but the crazy thing is I remember all our memories rather than our disagreements. Thank you for the heartbreak, Lord knows I needed to reach my lowest point before reaching my high. This next middle point is for you because you're one of the strongest people I've ever met.

Hiatus

The woman who has caught my eye is like a light

She often forgets how to show emotion

I want to hold and squeeze her with all my might

One look and you get lost in her eyes like the ocean

So many men gave her a grim feeling

She's contemplating who to trust

There're other ways to reach her than just sexual healing

They're chipping away at her heart like it's rust

Can't be ashamed of the past

I must look past all her flaws

Must make these final memories last

Love is an addiction, and I keep having withdraws

Her beauty has me under the greatest spell

So, I'm all in throwing my coins in this wishing well

Aftermath

Some of you are probably wondering by now how can I name a chapter after Hennessy and not talk about it. The background story of Hennessy and I came around my sophomore year when my boy Tyree bought a bottle into our dorm. Never experiencing Hennessy before I think the name alone captivated us. In college, everyone has the basic beer, vodka, twisted teas, and Mike's hard but there's something about when you walk into a party with a bottle of Henny that makes everyone stop and look at you with a glimpse of admiration and concern at the same time. There're different levels to this bottle of cognac for every occasion. If you're looking for a good time three – four shots will put you in the zone. If you're going through a heartbreak, I promise a personal bottle of Hennessy and Drake's Marvin's Room playing in the background will make the pain just a little better. If you're attempting to impress someone pull this bottle out and let them know you have a top-shelf taste. Hennessy is a part of the culture if you go to any club, a Black family cookout, or graduation party it will be right there welcoming you with open arms. Hopefully, I can get sponsored one day after all the money I spent over the years. Don't worry no alcoholic beverages were consumed during the making of this chapter. I wanted to experience every emotion that this chapter would give me. From the anger of ignorant people to the laughs that I had with my boys and to the acceptance of letting people you love go.

We Learned What?

Without struggle, there is no progress. -Frederick Douglass

At times I question myself and say how did I fall for the oldest trap in the book. In which I mean if I didn't attend college, I would be a bum or a failure — not realizing that I'm the one who controls my destiny. As kids, we're told if you go to college, you will get a job and live a good life. That might've been true 30 plus years ago, but today as our world continues to grow what does a college degree really get us? Let that marinate in your brain for a minute while I give you my reasoning. I believe college is a safety net for most people. I say that because after your 10th grade year of high school what do you learn that you didn't know previously? You see we go to college to perfect a craft, almost like a trade school. If you exclude the loud screaming commercials that come on during a commercial break of a Jerry Springer episode, replace that with your family members and teachers on the daily telling you to attend college. You see those kids who opt out of attending college are not all just buying time. They just understood that school was no longer for them. Working as a garbage truck driver, EMT specialist, welder, and police officer are all excellent quality jobs that you didn't need to attend college for.

In most cases, these people are making the same if not more money than our public-school teachers, which is crazy. Not crazy that these men and women make good money, but ridiculous that the people who are responsible for educating our youth are making the same amount as someone who didn't attend college. Our educators get paid like crap, and we wonder why kids nowadays can't even write their names in cursive. Some of you say it's not all about the money, it's about the love for the kids.

Well if that was true why is it when the first day of school comes around after any break parents are practically throwing their kids out the house? If parents don't even want their children at home what makes you think getting $40,000 is enough to keep 25 kids in classroom motivated long enough to pass a state test that is rigged for them to fail? And that's me being generous with the pay rate and understanding that I was able to attend one of the best liberal arts colleges in the Midwest taught me that I knew more than I thought. I majored in Communication and Rhetorical Studies, and after my four years, my speaking and writing skills sharpened. I perfected my craft, and it didn't teach me how to dissect a cat or how to do someone's taxes because that's not what I majored in. So why does it take four years? Honestly, it's for the experience. Between the ages of 17-22, you will probably have the biggest maturity jump in your life. I decided to continue my education career to keep perfecting my craft. As much as I dislike school sometimes, like Miami rapper, Ice Berg said "I'm chest deep in this sh*t" so there's no quitting until I reach my goal. My parents have put too much money in my education to be average… I hope to be Dr. Hicks one day. Be the professor that students from other majors want to take because I teach things that can be used in everyday life. I want to be wealthy, not rich. My goals are so close yet so far. You must ask yourself at night when you're alone, what's your goal?

Da Crib University

If you don't remember in previous chapters, I essentially said I'm from da crib, which refers to Miami, Dade County, Homestead to be exact. Whenever I went home for Christmas break and were around people who stayed at home, it was like time slowed down and that month being back felt like an eternity because I was living in two different worlds from my high school classmates. We just saw the world; differently, they had to mature a little bit quicker than most college kids because they were at the start of their careers at 18 or 19. I guess they figured that their chances of going to college were over, but that's not the case at all. You can always go back to school, but I remember what one of my advisors said during a summer internship, "Any 18-year-old kid can be a social media director for a company. You don't need a college degree; you need experience." This stood out to me because what she said was true. Every kid of this generation could run a successful social media account for a significant company, and college can't teach you something that comes naturally. I had classmates in undergrad that pursued careers that needed no college experience whatsoever, and they found themselves being in debt because of it. One of my classmates wanted to be a real estate agent... that took no college experience at all. My homeboy Denis is a certified personal trainer/real estate agent, and he is self-taught. He understood that in some career fields you must go out there and get it for yourself. For my readers contemplating whether to attend college or not, take your time with the decision because it's not the end of the world if you decide not to go. There are plenty of people who didn't attend college that are successful. If you work at Subway be the best employee Subway ever had because, in the long run, you can move up in the company and potentially run your own chain of Subways. Understanding that it doesn't matter what path you choose if you stick with it. I knew this girl in high school who dropped out and had two children by the age of 20. She knew that she had to provide for her family and she went back for her high school diploma and is working as an EMT. Find your Why in life.

Pinnacle

Earlier in the chapter, I referred to college as a safety net. College allows many to prolong being a kid while having adult responsibilities. When I was in my senior capstone class, I remember my professor asking everyone in class what their plans were after graduation and a good half of the class had no idea. The most significant misinterpretation of going to college is receiving a job. That couldn't be the further from the truth. Eighty-six percent of college grads stated that they were in a career job or a starter job leading to their career path. Of that 86 percent, 44 percent of college graduates work jobs that don't require a college degree. Now you understand why I stated kids are being brainwashed to attend college. Receiving your bachelor's is for the experience and memories. By the time you become a senior most are stressed and exhausted of school. You want to walk across that stage and shake the President's hand and never go back. While others hit that wall and understand that college has come to an end and they didn't learn anything. So, what do you learn in college? You learn the intangibles. You learn how to procrastinate until the last minute of a project. You're an accountant who can make $5 dollars stretch. You've become a certified nurse because you understand that drinking Pedialyte gets you over a hangover. All those failed attempts of being in someone's DM's has made you a communication major. Avoiding food in the cafeteria and making your own food saved you money on attending culinary school. Lying to your boyfriend or girlfriend to hang with your friends have given you the necessary tools of being a lawyer. Running student senate or being President of your organization has shown you that anyone can be a politician and I do mean anyone. These are the opportunities college blesses you with. Who knew in four years I practically majored in every subject that my undergrad offered.

#Adulting

"Much success to you, even if you wish me the opposite." –
Charlemagne Tha God

In writing this book, I had no idea what I was getting myself into. Honestly, nobody may even read it besides family and friends and I'm so grateful. The idea came around me wanting to give back to the youth. High school students get put into an auditorium in front of alumni and are expected to listen to others give their experiences on college. The volunteers who are giving these speeches aren't allowed to be entirely honest because what faculty member is going to let a guest speaker come and tell a group of girls that she was raped at a college party or that a minority student was called a racial slur. When have you known your high school to allow someone to come back who wasn't in college or famous? Nobody ever wants to let Michael who is a manager at Wendy's give his life experience except when it's job fair day. We brainwash our youth and rarely inform them of what reality is. The truth is, students are going to college and not coming out with jobs. We have a President in the White House who is letting everyone know racism is alive and well, that's popular belief. While the room for creativity in our classrooms are slowly fading away. I'm not an educator nor a politician. I'm just a realist. I understand at the young age of 23 that local drug dealers give back more to the community than the people who made it out successfully. I realize that no matter what education level I have, I will always have to work harder because of the color of my skin. I'm no longer that naïve kid who wishes he had super strength or super speed. I now know that being an educated Black man makes me one of the most dangerous people to come across. I wake up every day and ask the Lord to pray for me because no matter how much I abide by the rules, I'm just another ni**a. Places that used to be sacred are no longer safe anymore. Churches, schools, movie theatres and malls used to be off limits because this is where children would be mainly in attendance. When I think about having a family of my own, I am terrified of what the world has in store for them.

Selah

College will be the best and craziest times of your life, and it's something that you can't prepare for. The harsh reality is once you start getting in the flow of things, it's time to walk across the stage. For most, it's the last time you'll be on campus, and it is indeed the final goodbye with people you had the pleasure of knowing in your four years. Some meet the love of their lives, and others make friends that will be in their wedding one day. I got to meet my best friends, and I was able to meet a great man by the name of Joshua Hicks. Yes, I'm referring to myself because if college taught me anything, it taught me a lot about myself. No matter how hard you try, you can never outrun yourself or your thoughts. When you look in the mirror, you're the one who decides whether you made it in life. It doesn't matter how you get there; just matters that you finish. Most people blame not finishing college on grades, monetary reasons or family issues but who isn't in college going through at least one of those issues? The main reason why people don't finish is that they let themselves get in the way of succeeding. Writing this book has allowed me to reflect on my young adult life. Success is within us. I leave you with this, "Be strong and courageous. Do not be afraid; do not be discouraged, for the Lord your God will be with you wherever you go." Joshua 1:9